Baskets

Turning the Art of Making Beautiful Gift Baskets into a Profitable Business

How to Turn Your Passion into a Profitable Home-based Business

By

Laura Johnson

*Copyright © 2019 – **Valley Of Joy Publishing Press***

All Rights Reserved.

No part of this publication may be reproduced, stored in a retrieval system or transmitted in any form or by any means, electronic, mechanical, photocopying, recording or otherwise without the proper written consent of the copyright holder, except brief quotations used in a review.

Published by:

Valley Of Joy Publishing Press

Cover & Interior designed

By

Silvia Baker

First Edition

Contents

Part 1 Making Gift Baskets as a Hobby 3

    Introduction 3

Part 1 Chapter 1 Creating for Family and Friends 5

    Types of Baskets and Containers 6

    Shredding and Other Fillers 8

    Choosing a Theme and Selecting Products 9

    Tying Everything Together 10

    Purchasing Supplies on a Budget 12

Part 1 Chapter 2 Personalizing Your Gift Basket 15

    Spa and Pampering Gift Basket 17

    Teen Slumber Party Gift Goody Bags 19

    Sports Enthusiast Cooler Surprise 21

    Child's Fantasy Toy Land 23

Pet Lovers Treat Jar 25

Part 1 Chapter 3 Fabulous Gift Baskets on a Budget ... 27

Finding Inexpensive Baskets and Containers 27

Making Your Own Filler 29

Finding Inexpensive Products 31

Wrapping Your Creation 33

Finishing Touches 35

Part 1 Conclusion 37

Part 2 Building a Successful and Profitable Business ... 38

Introduction 38

Part 2 Chapter 1 Starting Your Business 40

Legal Considerations 40

Workspace and Inventory Management 43

Vendors for Products and Supplies 45

Part 2 Chapter 2 Advertising Your Business 48

Designing a Brochure 49

Networking and Social Media Marketing 51

Setting up a Website 54

Craft Fairs and Bazaars 55

Create a Sample Display 57

Create a Catalog Portfolio Album 59

Throw In-Home Parties 61

Conclusion 66

Glossary of Gift Basket Themes 68

Part 1 Making Gift Baskets as a Hobby

Introduction

Gift basket making is an extremely popular hobby.

I don't know anyone who doesn't love getting a basket filled with goodies as a gift. It is such a personal touch.

Almost everyone, at one time or another, has either made up or purchased a ready-made gift basket to give to a friend or family member on a special occasion. Maybe they made a breakfast basket for the couple that moved in next door to welcome them.

That basket might have included homemade cornbread in a cast iron skillet, orange marmalade in a glass jar, loose oranges, and a wrapped log of homemade butter.

Or perhaps it was a basket filled with fresh fruit, a soup mug, a container of homemade chicken soup, a tin of herbal teas, and warm fuzzy slippers for their sick best friend.

No matter what the occasion, if you are not already making gift baskets, this book will explain step by step how to make appealing and expensive looking gift baskets, inexpensively.

In this book, I am going to go even one step further for you. I will tell you how to turn that hobby of making gift baskets for just friends and family into a successful and profitable home-based business.

Part 1 Chapter 1 Creating for Family and Friends

There are many reasons for making rather than buying gift baskets. Gift baskets can get quite pricey to purchase ready-made.

Making a gift basket gives your gift that personalized touch. A lot of people have creative sides to their personality and create gift baskets to enhance that creativity. A gift basket is a unique and appealing gift.

No matter what your reason, you do not have to be creative to make appealing gift baskets.

You just have to know a few simple things to craft a thoughtful and beautiful gift basket:

- what types of baskets or containers to use
- shredding and other fillers
- how to choose a theme
- selecting the right products to personalize your basket
- how to tie everything together to make an appealing gift

- how to purchase your supplies on a budget.

Types of Baskets and Containers

First, let's look at the baskets or containers you will need and where to purchase them.

When we think of making a gift basket, a picture forms in our mind of the typical traditional woven basket. However, that is no longer the case.

There is a multitude of containers one can use to make a gift basket.

When choosing the type of container to use, it should be something that all of the products will fit into.

The container should also be a good fit for the types of products you have chosen to give.

For instance, if you make a gift basket for your best friend who loves to garden, you might choose to use a small planter, watering can, or a miniature wagon for the container.

As a gift for the gourmet cook or person who loves to bake, mixing bowls, colanders, cast iron skillets, and serving bowls make excellent containers to decorate and fill with gifts.

The list for the types of containers that can be used for making unique gift baskets is endless.

Don't forget that you can still use the traditional woven basket. These come in all different shapes, sizes, and colors.

Shredding and Other Fillers

Choosing filler for a gift basket is relatively easy. There is so much to choose from.

Be sure to choose something that you particularity like and that fits in with the contents of the basket or the container. There is no right or wrong choice. It is simply a personal preference.

For example, you might decide on a combination of green and orange colored shredded tissue paper for a Thanksgiving gift basket.

How about red foam balls for a Valentine's basket?

Other examples of different types of fillers include packing straw, confetti, Easter grass, and shredded newspaper. The list is endless!

Or better yet, why not make your own filler?

Choosing a Theme and Selecting Products

Selecting the products to go into your gift basket is extremely important. The product selection is what gives your gift a personalized touch.

First, you need to choose a theme. Think about the person the gift is for.

- What are his or her hobbies?
- Do they like reading, fishing, hiking, gourmet cooking, golfing, gardening, or playing sports?
- Is there anything special they like to pamper themselves with such as chocolate, a day trip to the spa, a golf outing with friends, or a good cigar?

Let's say your best friend likes to spend time in the kitchen, creating gourmet dishes. You might choose a cooking theme for her birthday gift basket.

You could fill that basket with one or two specialty cookbooks, a bottle of cooking Sherry or wine, a variety of exotic herbs and spices, some mixing spoons and cooking utensils, and even a couple of oven mitts. The possibilities are endless.

Just choose a theme that fits your recipient's personality and lifestyle, and the products will fall right into place.

Tying Everything Together

Once you have selected the basket or container, the filler, chosen a theme, and selected the products, you are ready to tie everything together to finish off your creation and make it look appealing.

In my opinion, the best wrapping to use to finish your basket and make it look expensive and more appealing is cellophane tape. This wrap is transparent and gives your basket a more professional look.

You will also need curling ribbon, bows, or ornaments that go with your theme. I also often include a gift card.

To wrap your basket in cellophane, follow these steps.

Step 1: Simply set your creation in the center of the cellophane.

Step 2: Lift and hold the front and back of the wrap with one hand while using the other hand to gather the remaining wrap.

Step 3: Once it has been gathered to your satisfaction, use the curling ribbon to tie it off.

Step 4: If there is any excess wrap, fold it under and tape it to the bottom of the basket.

Step 5: Finally, add your bow or ornament and gift card. These can be added to hide the curling ribbon you used to tie off the cellophane.

Now you have a beautiful, personally created gift for your friend or family member. It is a special gift that they will remember for years to come.

Purchasing Supplies on a Budget

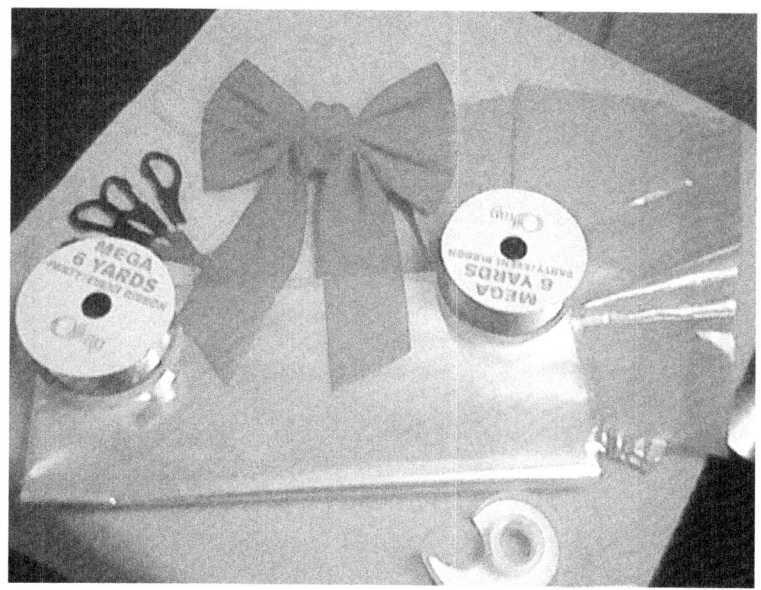

Buying gift basket supplies and products does not have to cost a fortune. You can make stylish and expensive looking gift baskets, even if you are on a budget.

Some of the best places to purchase baskets and different types of containers are dollar stores, thrift stores, yard sales, and even grocery stores. You will be pleasantly surprised at the really nice and stylish baskets and containers you can get for under $10 and even for only a $1 or $2.

Also, clean out your closets, garage, or attic. You never know what you might find stored away.

The same strategy applies to the purchase of fillers for your basket. You will find filler at the same types of stores that carry your baskets, many times on sale and at ridiculously low prices.

Another option is making your own filler. You can shred almost anything - old newspapers, magazines, and Christmas or birthday wrapping paper.

Many items you order come in boxes that are stuffed with wads of paper or popcorn filling. These make a great filler for gift basket containers. Again, the list is endless.

The rest of your needed supplies, such as bows and ornaments, can also be purchased at dollar stores, thrift stores, etc. You can sometimes find all the supplies you need for practically nothing at flea markets and yard sales.

Another man's junk could truly be your treasure. You just need to shop around a bit.

In regards to products to fill the basket, it is a personal choice about how much to spend on those items. You may want to find products you need on sale or go for the more expensive ones.

It is your creation and your gift for that special person. You decide how much you want to spend on them.

If you are on a limited income, you can find a multitude of products on sale in discount stores like Walmart or Target. Amazon is a great place to shop for products, and if you have Prime, you can buy with free shipping.

This is your creation, you set the spending limits, but know that you can make a professional, expensive looking creation for a lot less than it would cost to buy a ready-made gift basket in the store or online.

Part 1 Chapter 2 Personalizing Your Gift Basket

Anyone can purchase a ready-made gift basket from almost any online or regular retail store.

Granted, you can find some unique and beautiful baskets in the stores, but they are usually quite pricey.

So why not make your own gift basket for that special person in your life.

You will not only save money but can give a gift with a personalized touch that will be remembered for years to come.

In chapter one, I explained about choosing a theme and selecting the right products for that special recipient.

Now, let's take a look at what some of those themes and products might be and how to package them.

A few suggestions I have are:

- the spa and pampering gift basket
- teen slumber party fun goodie bags
- sports enthusiasts cooler surprise
- child's fantasy toy land
- pet lovers treat jar.

Spa and Pampering Gift Basket

What woman doesn't like to take time to pamper herself, whether in a spa or at home?

How about a spa night surprise birthday party?

Your guests bring the supplies they need to pamper themselves, and you provide the gift basket for your birthday friend, filled with spa pampering products.

Don't forget the snacks and drinks.

With good food, friends, and lots of "girl talk," it will be a birthday surprise that will be remembered for years to come.

Here are a few product suggestions to fill the spa pampering basket.

- use a foot tub as the container
- nail polish
- nail polish remover
- cotton swabs or balls
- bath salts and bombs
- nail file
- nail clippers
- toe separator
- facial and eye masks
- footstone and/or scrub
- a bottle of wine
- wine glasses
- candles.

The list is endless and only limited by your imagination.

Teen Slumber Party Gift Goody Bags

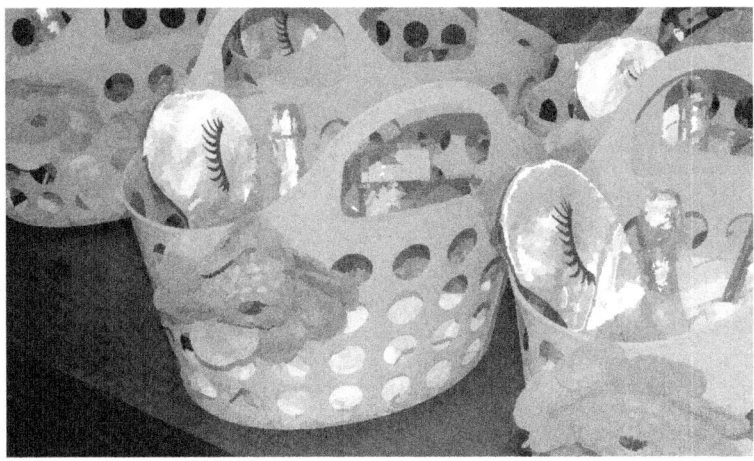

Is your daughter or niece turning sweet sixteen?

Have her invite 6 of her best friends over for a slumber birthday party!

Use a large pink gift bag filled with surprises for the birthday girl and smaller pink gift bags filled with surprises for the overnight guests.

The bags for the guests can contain items such as:

- an adult coloring book
- colored pencils
- gel pens

- hair ties
- friendship bracelets
- candy
- gum

For the birthday girl, put the same products as the guests, but add a few extras like:

- nail polish and remover
- cotton swabs or balls
- nail file
- nail clippers
- age appropriate music CD's
- iTunes gift card
- hairbrush and comb set
- cute socks
- chocolate or candies
- earbuds or headphones
- anything else you know she wishes for.

Don't forget the snacks and soda or fruit drinks and have some board games on hand.

It will be a fun night for all of the girls.

Sports Enthusiast Cooler Surprise

Most men are great sports enthusiasts.

I have a very special friend who spends every Tuesday on the golf course with three of his best golfing buddies.

One year on his birthday, I surprised him with what I call the "sports enthusiast cooler surprise."

In his case, it was the "golfer's delight" gift basket set.

You can really customize this set with any sort of sports related or hobby stuff for the special guy in your life.

I got a medium size Styrofoam cooler and filled it with

- ice
- cans of his favorite beer
- gift certificates for four sandwiches at Subway
- chips and dip
- a dozen new golf balls
- a package of golf tees
- a couple of golf towels
- a brand-new pair of golf shoes

Of course, I put the non-food gifts in a gift bag and put that in a waterproof container.

Needless to say, he was surprised and thrilled at the thoughtfulness.

You can do the same thing for a football, baseball, basketball, or any other type of sports fan.

Child's Fantasy Toy Land

Let's face it; children love toys. It doesn't matter how many toys they already have; they always want more.

As a container, you can find any number of things to use:

- large toys
- dump trucks
- small wagons
- beach buckets
- large gift bags.

Fill the container with a wide variety of toys.

For a boy, you might get:

- Legos
- plushies
- Xbox games
- Game Stop gift certificates
- card games like Uno
- matchbox cars.

Find out what he wishes for and add that if possible.

For girls you can add:

- dolls with a change of clothes
- pretend makeup
- sparkly bracelets
- colorful stickers
- coloring books
- crayons
- storybooks.

You might want to choose a large pink gift basket for that little one.

No matter what you choose, they will be sure to love getting a bag or other container filled with surprises.

Pet Lovers Treat Jar

Many of our friends and family today have pets.

These special animals are a part of their family, so let's not forget about them on special occasions.

Christmas is a wonderful time to remember pets.

A large mason jar makes a great gift jar to fill with treats for that special pet.

You could put the jar in a medium size Christmas gift bag and finish filling the bag with dog or cat toys.

If you aren't familiar with the pet personally, you may want to ask the owner what sorts of treats their pet loves or is able to have.

It is a lovely gesture and inexpensive enough to make one for all those people on your Christmas list who have pets.

Part 1 Chapter 3 Fabulous Gift Baskets On a Budget

Making gift baskets to give friends and family does not have to cost a fortune. You can make unique and expensive looking gift baskets on a budget or even on a fixed income.

This chapter will explore some of the ways you can make affordable creations that look expensive by finding inexpensive baskets and containers, making your own filler, wrapping your creation in cellophane, knowing where to find inexpensive and even free products, and making your own bows.

Finding Inexpensive Baskets and Containers

Gift baskets are still very popular. The container you choose should be unique and suitable for the number and types of products you plan to put into the container.

Remember that an ideal and appealing gift basket will appear to be overflowing with products and other goodies.

Suggestions for containers to use other than the traditional woven basket, depending on your theme are:

- tubs
- basins
- watering cans
- planters
- decorative pails
- miniature wagons
- sand pails
- dump trucks
- toy wagons
- serving bowls
- mixing bowls

The list goes on and on! Just use your imagination to decide what goes best with your theme and products.

The best place to shop for inexpensive traditional woven baskets and unique containers are dollar stores, yard and garage sales, flea markets, grocery stores, and discount warehouses.

Don't forget to check your closets and garage. You may find some containers and baskets that you stored and forgot about.

Ask family and friends if they have any baskets or containers that they are not using and wanting to get rid of. You do not have to spend a fortune to get baskets and containers. It may take a little cleaning or even some spray paint, but it is worth it in the long run.

Making Your Own Filler

When putting together a gift basket, you need filler to tuck into the corners and areas where there is nothing in the container.

The filler is also used for cushioning to keep the products from bumping against each other. It gives the final creation an overall fuller look.

Some fillers can be:

- crinkle cut paper shred fillers
- bags of mini Styrofoam balls
- packing peanuts.

Numerous other fillers can be purchased in bulk online, at retail craft stores, and discount warehouses.

Wouldn't it be better to get your filler for free? You can simply make your own.

If you do not have a shredder at home, see if you can borrow one from a friend or family member. If not, then use a sharp pair of scissors to cut the strips.

You can use:

- old newspapers (ask friends and family to save theirs for you)
- last year's leftover Christmas wrapping paper
- brown paper bags
- glossy paper from advertising fliers
- colored thin construction
- printer paper
- any used paper
- leftover Easter grass.

It is time-consuming to cut the paper into strips, but the money you save will make it worthwhile in the long run.

Finding Inexpensive Products

When you are ready to purchase the gifts/products for your creation, there are a variety of avenues open for buying them on a budget or fixed income. Some products you can even get for free.

Once you choose your theme around that one special gift for your recipient, it is easy to fill the rest of the basket with free and inexpensive products.

Check out your local dollar stores and discount warehouses. Even grocery stores carry a multitude of items besides food. Be sure to check the sale bins and 'buy one, get one' specials.

In today's society, large local flea market vendors carry new items at ridiculously low prices. I once picked up a dozen baskets in different shapes, colors, and sizes for 25 cents each at our weekend flea market. I was also able to stock up on make-up, books, and DVDs at fabulous prices, most less than a dollar each.

Don't forget about eBay and Amazon. You can sometimes find incredible buys on these sites with free shipping.

As for those free products, there are lots of companies that will send you free samples of their products if you just ask.

Send them an email or make a phone call. Let them know you want to try before you buy.

There is also a ton of websites on the internet that will help you get free product samples in the mail.

And of course, keep an eye out for the 'buy one get one free' products.

BOGO does not just apply to food at the grocery store.

You may spend a little extra time getting everything you want, but it is worth the effort, in the long run, to fill up that basket.

Wrapping Your Creation

Now it's time to wrap that full basket and add the finishing touches with a bow and gift card.

Even though some people have used clear plastic wrap or plastic bags to wrap homemade gift baskets, it is not something I would recommend. It makes the basket look really cheap.

Transparent or cellophane tape is ideal for wrapping your basket. It makes the basket look more professional, is inexpensive, and is easy to use.

You can purchase large rolls, usually 30-40 in x 100 ft for less than $20. That is enough to wrap several baskets of different sizes.

Do not skimp on the wrap. The cellophane gives any gift basket a great professional look. Your inexpensive gift will now look expensive.

When you wrap, make sure to size your basket and cut enough cellophane to make a nice gather at the top of the basket.

Please refer back to Chapter 1 for instructions on how to wrap the basket.

Now you are ready to add a bow and gift card.

Finishing Touches

The final touch to this beautiful personalized gift creation is adding a bow or other topper and a gift card.

Using a good quality satin bow can make all the difference in the world in the look of your basket. It can turn something unsightly into a rich, lush, and stylish creation.

You can find satin ribbon for around 59 cents per yard for 1 1/2-inch ribbon. Two yards will be more than enough for a few of the largest baskets.

Now to make the bow.

Instead of writing out step by step instructions, I think a visual would be more effective. So, I am giving you a link where you can find a great video on how to make a beautiful bow for the finishing touches.

You can even get some ribbon and follow along.

You will be amazed at how incredibly simple it is to make such a fabulous looking bow.

Just go to this link, and you will find the video on YouTube, "How to Make a Bow for a Wrapped Gift Basket" (https://www.youtube.com/watch?v=w9FO281y-64).

Once your bow is done, add your gift card. You have crafted a beautiful and expensive looking gift basket for just pennies on the dollar.

Part 1 Conclusion

In Part 1 of this book, I have explored making gift baskets for family and friends as a fun hobby and way to save money.

I covered the types of containers to use, where to find inexpensive supplies and products, themes to choose, and even making your own shredded fillers and lovely bows.

In chapter 2, I am going to tell you how to take that hobby and turn it into a fun, creative, and professional profit-making business.

After reading Part 1, hopefully, you are excited about making gift baskets for your family and friends.

It's time to turn that creativity and enthusiasm from a hobby into a profitable and successful business venture.

Part 2 Building a Successful and Profitable Business

Introduction

Gift baskets are extremely popular. They can be found online or in your local retail stores.

Just do a Google search for "gift baskets," and you will be amazed at what you'll find.

Don't be intimidated by the variety. Competition is good, and you will be turning your hobby into a local "customized" business.

Part 2 of this book is going to cover the basics of starting a business. We know it's going to be a business producing customized gift baskets, so the information will be geared to that type of home-based business.

Chapter 1 will cover the legalities of setting up your business, defining your gift basket market, choosing your workspace, locating your product and supply vendors, and an alternative to stocking inventory.

Chapter 2 is all about advertising and promotion.

You will learn how to design brochures, conduct local and online networking, social media marketing, the basics of setting up a website, and the advantages of attending craft fairs and bazaars.

By the end of the book, you will be ready to sell your gift baskets.

I will give you suggestions for themes to use, holiday promotions, open houses, business to business marketing, word of mouth, and even setting up in-home parties.

The conclusion will summarize all I have touched on in Part 2 and will have website links for you to check out.

I will also provide a list of at least 50 themes you can use to customize your gift baskets.

Let your imagination continue to add to that list.

Part 2 Chapter 1 Starting Your Business

Once you make the decision to turn your gift basket making hobby into a business, there are several important issues to consider. Please note the following steps necessary to set up your business legally.

Legal Considerations

Pick a name and type of entity. If you are in business alone, a sole proprietorship is probably best.

Please consult an attorney or the Small Business Administration (SBA). You can find them online at https://www.sba.gov/.

You probably already have a name in mind, but if not, no sweat. You can always ask friends and families for ideas.

If you are on Facebook, post a contest to "Name that Business." Whoever submits the winning name will receive a free gift basket. The prize could be redeemed now or at a later date.

This suggestion is two-fold. It gives you a name for your business and promotes your up-and-coming new business venture.

You could also offer a $5.00 off gift certificate to everyone who submits a name by email. That will be a plus, as now you have an email subscription mailing list.

Obtain a federal tax ID number (EIN). EIN or Employer Identification number is essentially a social security or tax identification number but for your business.

You can apply for an EIN online at https://www.irs.gov/businesses/small-businesses-self-employed/how-to-apply-for-an-ein.

Make sure to get all of the proper licenses. Once again, you can check with an attorney, the SBA, or your local county licensing office.

Make sure to get your business registered with the proper sales tax agencies. Since you will be selling your baskets retail, you will need to collect and pay local and possibly state sales tax. This may require a "seller's permit" depending on your state's regulations.

It is important to make sure you set up your business within the legal guidelines. Do the research based on your state where you plan to do business.

Open a business bank account. It is best not to mix personal and business finances. You want to know exactly what is coming in and going out of your business. It will definitely make things a lot easier at tax time, especially if you have someone else prepare your taxes.

I strongly recommend that you consult an attorney to obtain all legal requirements for setting up a small home-based business in your location.

You can also simply go the website for your particular county or state and find all the legal information you need. Some county and state sites even have applications you can fill out and allow you to pay license fees online.

Utilize the Small Business Administration (SBA). They will walk you through everything you need to know. The SBA can even connect you with attorneys and free business counselors to get you started. Be sure to you take all the necessary steps necessary to open and run your business legally.

Workspace and Inventory Management

Now that you have the legal stuff out of the way, it's time to choose your workspace.

You can actually work in any room in your house or apartment. You will only need a room or area that has a table. You could even set up a card table to work on. You do not need a big area because you will not need a large inventory to begin your business.

I would suggest making only 1 or 2 finished baskets, each with a different theme. The reason behind this is because you are going to have a customized gift basket business. Your baskets will be made to order.

You will advertise what you can make, suggesting themes depending on the occasion or individual recipient's tastes. Then you will consult with your client and find out what they need and how much they are willing to spend.

You don't want to make a basket and spring a price on them that is over their budget. They will either purchase the products to put in the basket or can pay you to do the shopping.

You will settle on the theme and a price depending on what they order for their specific budget. You will take a deposit and make the basket within a time frame you have both agreed upon.

Ultimately, you will not need to stock much inventory in the beginning. Concentrate on one order at a time. Don't overwhelm yourself. Hopefully, your business will grow, and you can hire others to help.

Make sure to take photos of every basket you complete. Put these in a really nice album. The album will showcase the beautiful baskets you have made. It can be used as a sales tool (like a portfolio) to show off your work.

Vendors for Products and Supplies

As I mentioned earlier, since this will be a customized business, you will not need to stock a large inventory. Therefore, initially, you can save a lot of money.

It's all about themes. Locate your local vendors that sell baskets, tape, cellophane, ribbon, and all the basic supplies you regularly use.

Also, keep in mind that your client may want you to purchase the product to fill the basket. Make sure to take a large enough deposit to cover such up-front purchases and be sure to keep all of your receipts.

Visit some smaller specialty shops and talk with the managers or owners. Introduce yourself and leave business cards or brochures with everyone.

Have a couple of specialty shops in mind for items but don't forget about your local Walmart or Target for product purchases.

At some point, the managers of these specialty stores may even let you leave one or two baskets on display. Work out a reasonable percentage to offer the owner or manager for any sales made from the display.

You can purchase basket making supplies from dollar stores, discount stores, and craft stores. Even some fabric stores have baskets, ribbon, tape, and decorative items.

Don't forget about flea markets and yard sales. Some of my best baskets came from these for pennies on the dollar.

Talk to friends and family members. They may have baskets they are not using and even left-over tape or ribbons.

You never know what they have until you ask and free is always good. You can purchase a plastic storage bin to keep your supplies in and put your baskets in a closet or a second storage bin.

Part 2 Chapter 2 Advertising Your Business

In part 2, chapter 1 of this book, you learned the legalities for setting up your home-based gift basket making business. You now know how and where to create and set up your workspace. You have a better understanding of where to look for your supplies, what supplies you need to get started, and how much to keep on hand.

Part 2, chapter 2, is going to delve into the best way to advertise your custom gift baskets even on a budget. You will learn about designing brochures and business cards.

You will also learn about local and online networking, social media marketing, and the basics of setting up your own website, Facebook business page, or group site.

You will discover the advantages of in-home parties. The strategy of utilizing home parties is virtually untouched in this market.

We'll talk about exploring, networking at, and signing up for booths with local craft fairs, and bazaars.

Let's get started by learning about an important advertising tool - a colorful brochure.

Designing a Brochure

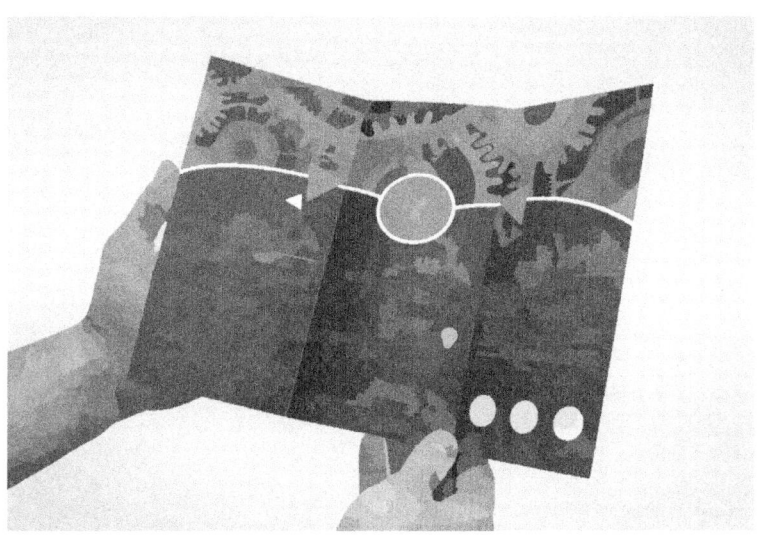

One of the most important tools for advertising your custom gift baskets is a professional looking and colorful brochure.

This will be invaluable when attending networking events, going business to business (B2B), and having on a display stand on your table at local craft shows and bazaars.

Design a brochure and attach a matching personalized business card with all of your contact information. You can leave these at the doctor's office, dentist, local florists, bridal shops, your hairdresser, insurance agency, bank, or anywhere else you do business.

Keep enough in your car to leave 2 or 3 in each place where you do business or shop.

For the actual design, you can save a ton of money by doing it yourself online.

Free templates can be found on websites like Vistaprint, Wix, Adobe Spark, and even on Microsoft Office 365 if you have a subscription. If you do not have a subscription to Microsoft Office 365, I recommend Vistaprint. They are reasonable and easy to use.

You can design the brochure and matching personal card, and they print the number you specify and send them to you. You can start for as little as $20 for brochures and the same amount for business cards.

Also, watch for sales. I recently got 500 business cards for $9.99 plus shipping. However, if you have a good color printer, you can use any free printable template from the internet and print your own brochures and personal cards. It's your choice.

When designing your brochure, make sure to have pictures of at least two different themed gift baskets.

Make sure you specify that these are customized gift baskets made to order.

Include pricing and deposit information, such as indicating you require 50% down and the rest of the balance paid upon delivery.

Research gift baskets online. Send off for brochures. Get some ideas but put those ideas into your own words. Brochures are important advertising tools, and they are simple to make.

Networking and Social Media Marketing

Now let's talk about local and online networking and social media marketing.

Business networking, by definition, is establishing a mutually beneficial relationship with other local business people and potential clients and customers.

Networking is an essential part of any successful home-based business. Your goal is to meet potential clients or generate referrals.

You can network in your local community by attending local craft shows, bazaars, and flea markets. Find local business networking groups and then be continually active in the group by attending their meetings and functions.

A good resource for finding local groups to network with is Meetup.com (https://www.meetup.com/). You can join a local group as a female entrepreneur, as a home-based business owner, or as a minority-owned business – whatever situation applies to you. There are tons of specific groups you can search for and join via this app.

However, pace yourself. Don't join more groups than you have time to participate in actively. You need to make sure to keep enough time free to work your business.

In regards to social media marketing, find group sites that allow you to advertise and post links to your website. Upload your brochure.

You might want to start a blog about gift basket making. There are plenty of sites where you can establish a blog for free.

Join LinkedIn and Twitter. You will probably be surprised at how many people in your local area are members of Facebook, LinkedIn, and Twitter. Don't overwhelm yourself and join more groups than you can keep up with.

To recap for social media marketing: join Facebook, Twitter, LinkedIn, and consider starting a blog.

Locally, find one or two networking groups to join. Attend meetings and functions to meet other business people.

Don't forget to take brochures and personal business size cards with you everywhere you go.

You might even donate a gift basket as a door prize for a local organization's meeting or function. This will showcase your creativity and help boost sales.

Everyone you connect with is a potential client. Don't be shy; ask them for at least one referral. Word of mouth is the best way to grow your business!

Setting up a Website

Since you are going to establish a customized local business, setting up a website is not urgent.

However, with that being said, your local clients can certainly recommend you to their friends and family by word of mouth or on social media.

Having an established website can be a distinct advantage.

If you are not technically savvy, there are any number of hosting sites that can help you set up a website or even design and set one up for you for a fee.

Put in a little research time and find the host that suits your specific needs for your business.

Craft Fairs and Bazaars

A huge boost to your business can come from word of mouth, happy customers, and networking.

Start attending local craft fairs and bazaars. Look for vendors who sell gift baskets.

You can get ideas and inspiration from your competition. Talk to them and exchange business cards. You might be able to help each other at some point down the road.

Remember, every vendor you meet is a potential customer, and they all have friends, family, and contacts.

Once you get some sample baskets ready, become a vendor at craft fairs or bazaars.

Display your sample baskets, your brochures, and business cards.

You could host a giveaway for a custom gift basket. The more valuable the prize, the better response you will get.

Have registration forms that include name, address, phone number, and email address of the person entering the drawing.

When these are filled out, they will give you potential future customers and an addition to your email contact list.

Make sure to post the time that the drawing will be held.

This will bring people back to your table and remind them of you and what you sell.

You could easily go home from the event with a few orders and definitely a large number of names and email addresses of potential customers.

Create a Sample Display

You have learned enough of the basics to get started with your own customized gift basket home-based business.

You are going to need to know how to work with your clients to explain and show them what you can create. You may need to help guide them in choosing the perfect gift basket for that special someone in their life.

To begin with, create at least four to six baskets for display in the area where you will be working with your clients. You might want to invest in a long folding table such as you would use at a craft fair for your basket display.

Make sure to cover it with a plain, but colorful tablecloth. Something patterned or too gaudy will be a distraction from your baskets. Your baskets should be the focal point, not the tablecloth.

Be sure to showcase baskets of different shapes, sizes, and colors. Choose a different theme for each basket.

Put a place card beside each basket that that is printed with the theme and price of that particular basket.

Make sure your client understands their price may vary depending on the basket and type and number of products they choose.

Fill each basket with six to eight products relating to the theme you have chosen.

From time to time, a client may decide to purchase your ready-made basket on display. That is great! Simply create another one to replace it.

If you sit down with a pen and paper, you could probably brainstorm an endless list of themes on your own. You can ask friends and family for ideas.

Create a Catalog Portfolio Album

In the glossary at the end of this book, I am going to help you get started by giving you a list of themes I have researched.

A few of these themes I list I have used in my own business. This list by no means will cover everything, but it is a good place to start for something to show to your clients.

I mentioned in a previous chapter that you should take pictures of the baskets you create for displays. You can purchase an inexpensive and attractive photo album to use for your pictures.

The list of themes you type up can be inserted in this album along with any pictures you take. Always take pictures of every basket you make for a client or for display.

Eventually, you will have a beautiful portfolio filled with pictures of your creations, suggested themes, prices, your brochure, and a personalized business card.

Don't forget to get testimonials from your satisfied clients to add to the portfolio. All you will have to do is sit down with your prospective client, and the catalog will make the sale for you.

This list of themes is to assist those clients that are not sure what type of basket they want. Your client may already have an idea or know what products they want in their gift basket.

If not, you can provide a list for them to look over. You may also need to help them select gifts to correspond with their theme. Make sure to read over any theme list you add to your album so you will know how to advise the client.

Throw In-Home Parties

Everyone loves a party, right?

Home party businesses have been quite successful. Most of us can remember family members holding parties for selling makeup or food containers at their homes.

Everyone gets together at one person's home where there are food, drinks, and a host or hostess. There is brand new, interesting, and shiny merchandise on display for sale.

For your basket business, invite some of your contacts you have made to your house. Have door prizes for the guests, plenty of brochures, business cards, and baskets on display for immediate sale. Set up your display and have your portfolio catalog on hand.

Consider giving your guests some party favors because everyone loves free stuff. You could coordinate with other home-based business owners to offer their products in promotion at your party in exchange for free samples or something you can offer your guests. This type of partnership is key to your networking.

Home parties can even be held at local restaurants or coffee shops. Find a location that has an event room or a party room that you can reserve for free or if you purchase the food for the party with the venue. This can also make clean up easier for you.

Prepare a short sales-pitch talk, but don't spend the whole time talking. Don't bore your guests. Give a quick testimony of why you started this business. Be sure to thank everyone for attending.

Briefly outline what you offer and how it can benefit your guests. Describe some of the inventory you have for sale now and that you can take orders during the party. Especially highlight anything new or exciting for your business.

Notify your guests if you'll be at any craft shows or fairs in the near future so they can bring their friends to see your baskets in person. Advertise if you have any upcoming raffles or giveaways and how they can enter them. Brag about if your gift baskets have been donated to organizations for their fundraising efforts.

Make it a social occasion. Serve food and drinks. Help the guests mingle, talk about themselves, and encourage conversation. Consider playing an icebreaker game to get the guests talking.

It's fun to have a theme for the party – maybe with a display of baskets to coordinate with the theme.

One idea may be that during wedding season (usually May and June), invite ladies only and make it themed as if it were a wedding shower where every female guest is the (pretend) bride-to-be!

You can play wedding shower type games, serve cake, and provide your guests with a corsage or flower to wear.

All the while, reminding them of the basket packages you can create that can be special gifts for the actual brides they may visit this season.

For instance, you might create a "Kitchen Essentials" basket with various kitchen gadgets.

This type of basket could be for a newly married woman or someone setting out on their own (think graduation season, too).

Ask your party guests to recommend 2-3 friends whom you can contact with your marketing materials.

Ask them to give you their friends email address or phone number to generate leads.

Offer incentives to your guests for providing you with leads.

Finally, before your party ends, be sure to book another party with at least one of your guests to be hosted at their house.

Offer incentives to the new party hostess, such as discounts or a percentage of the sales generated at her party.

Suggest that a basket party would be a good idea for birthdays, anniversaries, weddings, graduations, baby showers, housewarming parties – any special occasion where the gifts purchased could be purchased for the hostess in addition to the guests' personal purchases.

Conclusion

Now you have a decision to make.

If you are already making gift baskets for a hobby, do you want to turn that hobby into a profitable business?

Whether you decide just to make gift baskets as a hobby or open your own customized gift basket home-based business, I have given you more than enough information to get you up and running.

In this book, I showed you how to:

- How to craft fabulous gift baskets
- Where to source cheap materials
- How to start selling baskets as a business venture
- How to market those baskets
- Tips for how to make gift baskets special and unique
- How to throw an in-home basket party
- Encouragement to strike out on your own!

Making gift baskets for friends and family or even clients to give to others is creative, fun, and rewarding.

Thank you for purchasing my book. I hope you enjoyed reading it as much as I enjoyed writing it for you.

If you have gotten something from the advice in this book, would you please consider leaving a review wherever you purchased this book? I value your feedback.

Best of luck to you as you begin your venture into the world of gift basket making!

Glossary of Gift Basket Themes

1. Pamper Mom
2. Surprise Dad
3. Golfer's Accessories
4. Fisherman's Catch
5. Romantic Night Out
6. Book Lover
7. Sports Enthusiast
8. Chocolate Lover's Delight
9. Baker's Bowl
10. 50 and Fabulous
11. College Survival Kit
12. Pretty in Pink
13. Crafter
14. Candles, Candles, and More Candles
15. Baby Shower
16. A Day at the Beach
17. Outdoor Adventurer
18. Welcome Home
19. Welcome to the Neighborhood
20. A Green Thumb
21. Sweet 16
22. Antique Lover

23. Mother's Day
24. Father's Day
25. Grandparent's day
26. For Dogs Only
27. For Cats Only
28. Child's Fantasy Toyland
29. Wedding Shower
30. Family Game Night
31. Family Movie Night
32. Favorite Teacher
33. Gourmet Chef
34. Weekend Getaway
35. Coffee Lover's Delight
36. Bosses Day
37. Secretary's Day
38. Soldier's Treats from Home
39. Italian Dinner Night
40. Mexican Fiesta Night
41. Chinese Buffet Night
42. Photo Shoot
43. Art Enthusiast Package
44. Graduation Day
45. Carpenter's Bag of Tools
46. Merry Christmas
47. Gamers Fun Package

48. Computer Geek's Treats
49. First Day of School
50. Happy Valentine's Day

Printed in Great Britain
by Amazon